W9-BBQ-277

liquid damage noted 7/20 09

DATE DUE

| | |
|---|---|
| APR 0 7 2002 | FEB 2007 |
| APR 1 6 2002 | AUG 0 7 2002 |
| MAY 1 7 2002 | JAN 2 9 2003 |
| JUN 1 7 2002 | DEC 1 7 2011 |
| NOV 1 6 2001 | NOV 1 0 2002 |
| FEB 2 8 2012 | |

THE DISCARDED BY THE
URBANA FREE LIBRARY

(217) 367-4057

DISCARDED BY THE
URBANA FREE LIBRARY

# Nouns

THE URBANA FREE LIBRARY

TO RENEW MATERIALS CALL
(217) 367-4057

Kelly Doudna

*3/02*
*Center for children's books*

Published by SandCastle™, an imprint of ABDO Publishing Company, 4940 Viking Drive, Edina, Minnesota 55435.

Copyright © 2001 by Abdo Consulting Group, Inc. International copyrights reserved in all countries. No part of this book may be reproduced in any form without written permission from the publisher. SandCastle™ is a trademark and logo of Abdo Publishing Company.

Printed in the United States.

Photo credits: Comstock, Eyewire Images, PhotoDisc, Rubber Ball

Library of Congress Cataloging-in-Publication Data

Doudna, Kelly, 1963-
    Nouns / Kelly Doudna.
      p. cm. -- (Sentences)
    Includes index.
    ISBN 1-57765-614-8
     1. English language--Noun--Juvenile literature. [1. English language--Noun.] I. Title.

PE1201 .D67 2001
428.2--dc21

2001022891

The SandCastle concept, content, and reading method have been reviewed and approved by a national advisory board including literacy specialists, librarians, elementary school teachers, early childhood education professionals, and parents.

## Let Us Know

After reading the book, SandCastle would like you to tell us your stories about reading. What is your favorite page? Was there something hard that you needed help with? Share the ups and downs of learning to read. We want to hear from you! To get posted on the Abdo Publishing Company Web site, send us email at:

**sandcastle@abdopub.com**

# About SandCastle™

## Nonfiction books for the beginning reader

- Basic concepts of phonics are incorporated with integrated language methods of reading instruction. Most words are short, and phrases, letter sounds, and word sounds are repeated.

- Readability is determined by the number of words in each sentence, the number of characters in each word, and word lists based on curriculum frameworks.

- Full-color photography reinforces word meanings and concepts.

- "Words I Can Read" list at the end of each book teaches basic elements of grammar, helps the reader recognize the words in the text, and builds vocabulary.

- Reading levels are indicated by the number of flags on the castle.

*Note: Some pages in this book contain more than ten words in order to more clearly convey the concept of the book.*

## Look for more SandCastle books in these three reading levels:

| Level 1 (one flag) | Level 2 (two flags) | Level 3 (three flags) |
|:---:|:---:|:---:|
|  |  |  |
| **Grades Pre-K to K** 5 or fewer words per page | **Grades K to 1** 5 to 10 words per page | **Grades 1 to 2** 10 to 15 words per page |

# Nouns

A noun is a person, place, or thing.

# Nouns

My family and I build a snowman together.

# Nouns

I want a snack.

I will eat an apple.

# Nouns

I run on the beach.

The sand is soft.

11

# Nouns

We buy vegetables at the store.

# Nouns

I peek around the back of the chair.

# Nouns

My dad and I take pictures
with the camera.

# Nouns

I like to float in the pool in hot weather.

# Nouns

What nouns do you see in this picture?

(basket, girl, grass, rabbit)

# Words I Can Read

## Nouns

**A noun is a person, place, or thing**

apple (AP-UHL) p. 9
back (BAK) p. 15
basket (BASS-kit) p. 21
beach (BEECH) p. 11
camera (KAM-ur-uh) p. 17
chair (CHAIR) p. 15
dad (DAD) p. 17
family (FAM-uh-lee) p. 7
girl (GURL) p. 21
grass (GRASS) p. 21
noun (NOUN) p. 5
person (PUR-suhn) p. 5

picture (PIK-chur) p. 21
place (PLAYSS) p. 5
pool (POOL) p. 19
rabbit (RAB-it) p. 21
sand (SAND) p. 11
snack (SNAK) p. 9
snowman
  (SNOH-man) p. 7
store (STOR) p. 13
thing (THING) p. 5
weather (WETH-ur) p. 19

## Plural Nouns

**A plural noun is more than one
person, place, or thing**

nouns (NOUNZ) p. 21
pictures (PIK-churz) p. 17

vegetables
  (VEJ-tuh-buhlz) p. 13

# Verbs

**A verb is an action or being word**

**build** (BILD) p. 7
**buy** (BYE) p. 13
**do** (DOO) p. 21
**eat** (EET) p. 9
**float** (FLOHT) p. 19
**is** (IZ) pp. 5, 11
**like** (LIKE) p. 19

**peek** (PEEK) p. 15
**run** (RUHN) p. 11
**see** (SEE) p. 21
**take** (TAYK) p. 17
**want** (WONT) p. 9
**will** (WIL) p. 9

# Adjectives

**An adjective describes something**

**hot** (HOT) p. 19
**my** (MYE) pp. 7, 17

**soft** (SAWFT) p. 11
**this** (THISS) p. 21

23

# Match each picture to the noun that names it

**camera**

**chair**

**pictures**

**snowman**

24